ARIES CONSTELLATION

Aries Constellation

A collection of Poems

DANICIA ARMSTRONG

Danicia Armstrong

INTRODUCTION

Introduction

This is a collection of poems that I have put together while I was going through some very dark moments in my life. I have learned to write and read myself straight through everything that was once causing me to feel as if I was all alone, lost, and suffering within the world. It was a way to help me see what was happening to me when I felt like the only one that was unaware of these things and even though I may be at a strong place right now, I know things happen in life that may begin to shake and reshape our character. I talk about love, longing, loneliness, and what it means to stand strong as an individual. I also have some inspirational poems that I share because in order for me to remain in a peaceful state of mind, it is imperative that I read and write. It's like digging for diamonds with a pencil as my metaphorical shovel. I've written through heart aches and trauma that I still deal with regularly. This is how I let things go with love.

DEDICATION

Dedication

I dedicate this book to my family, my spiritual uncles at the Stars Bus station, my helpful instructors, the libraries and book stores I sat in for many hours, and my close friends. This book has been created while I dealt with some shameful attachments within my life. For a while I could not accept myself for who I was and I settled for people that did not appreciate who I am. Even though I could not see what was happening to me, I stood my ground and kept my character despite how I was beginning to be judged, abused, and unheard. These individuals would remind me that I was strong and even though I was clueless as to why they would randomly say this, I would thank them because part of me felt they believed in me and saw me for who I am inside and continued to motivate me. I know they saw the self-doubt right through the mask I'd wear. This is also a declaration of everything I love about myself. Even the strange complexities of which I have mistakenly neglected to see as beautiful. I forgive myself for that, so I have written this as a reminder that it is okay to share my colors. It is okay to share my story. This journey taught me to only share my story with those that are deserving of it, so if you are a healer, I write to you.

YOUNG AND DUMB

Young and Dumb

What is a good citizen?
What is it if you're too anxious to wait on a stop light,
or passing cars,
or even a clean space?
a happy place.
What are the rules that got me laced?

DEATH

Death

When the night falls, I call it a murder that typically goes unsolved.

It is a death in which I've continuously failed at trying to understand.

You see sometimes I have these dreams that are too big for me.

There's a night stand near my bed and on it I keep a journal.

Those journals hold so many things and sharing my dreams once broke my heart.

It even tried to kill my spirit.

I write because it brings me back to life like when Jesus resurrected right in front of his people.

I wake and crawl away into my space until I get hungry or night reminds me that morning is to come.

This idea of death tugs at the truth that there is work that still needs to be done.

We've done our best today; I occasionally say to myself just as a reminder to relax on most days.

Is it a dark night of the soul?

Perhaps it is.

BREAKING POINT

Breaking Point

Crying does not solve a single problem although the chemical balance I have in my mind caused by it washes over me like a misty breeze straight off the cost in the Middle East.

I've learned to arm myself from harm.

I pray and celebrate.

I did not know what happened.

I put on a face and tell myself the truth about the position I'm in.

Sometimes I dream of breaking away, but I refuse to make any moves just yet.

I still believe I have everything I need right in my little room.

I really have no place to fit, so I dig my way through.

The Earth's core even burns the same way I do.

I wonder why a lot.

The silence is nice; it reveals some of the darkest spots inside.

I begin to internalize all of the emotions as if they were telling my mind the truth.

It takes the form of pity and I make no room for it.

You're a smart girl; you'll make it through.

Thank you.

I have expectations that are limitless and perhaps I may have dreamt a tad bigger than I expected to.

I still fight my way through.

I tell myself "I'll stand alone if I have to."

Sometimes I fail at meeting expectations and maybe it's me or possibly the voices I've struggled to be.

People laugh, most are jealous, and to be quite frank, I barely remember their names let alone their faces.

A Glimpse of The Future

-Reality at its knees-

Is it enough to write faithfully;
To enjoy the complex nature of the way the pen curves.
To exhale at the end of each written word.
What more is to be said?
The future is bright and full of color.
Peace will be spread over the nation like a blanket of snow under a sled.
We're rainbows with smiles that glow and eyes that sparkle.
I see a glimpse of a future of men protecting their families.
I see a glimpse of the future where women are strong standing up on their own two feet.
There's a future that does not boast about unimportant things.
There's a future out there and I know it begins with me.
I know in time; I'll see myself for who I am and what I believe.

Little Lady

Dear young woman,
I'm talking to the ladies that love so hard.
The ones that see the good in those they love.
Stop believing you can save him.
Don't wait for him to show you love.
Open yourself up to it.
Dear young lady,
open your eyes.
Real love is felt every day.
People or things will seem like love, but it's really an expression of your reflection.
And no, I do not mean the one you see when you stare into the mirror for hours fixing yourself up to be rejected, neglected, and manipulated.
Harsh love? It's still love because I write with truth.
Put the phone down and raise up.
You're the divine power that helped God compile the mind up.
Dear young woman, wake up and allow yourself to be great.

2 a.m thoughts

It seems I am waiting for that moment I cannot resist a smile.

Is it the complexity of sadness if not happiness?

Words I hear through some days continue to whirl around in my brain.

I lay my head on a pillow gracefully accepting the course of today.

I have not written much lately.

My heart has been empty so it seems I am still searching for reasons to accept me.

I once roamed the land, running from weak and mentally unstable men that beg to take my hand.

I have seen that I cannot side with promiscuous women or men whom frivolously lay with any bodies, man.

I do not blame em though; the inside of us gets lonely especially when the only life one enjoys lives outside the flesh.

It sucks when we forget to be grateful.

I have seen many become unholy.

They are strong to me of course.

As for me,

I am afraid of going to parties or clubs that play music by fake thugs exploiting the women they once loved, wandering eyes and words at times.

I am a mess yet I fear dying less...

It is 2 a.m,

this is my rest.

Unjust Society

Why do we look at social media with greed in our eyes?

Have I also become blind?

I've grown tired of talking.

Everyone wants to hear from me, but I own them nothing.

Everything I say will be tested and held against me.

I'm tested, and on the verge of stressing.

Wait a minute.

I knew I was exposed since the beginning.

Everyone thought I did not know.

It's an unjust society.

"Ask for help."

Why on Earth would I set myself up to be victimized in that way?

Many people would label it as pride, but I refuse to believe that.

Asking for help with this has only kept me codependent on "help" that doesn't.

I was asking for help in a different kind of way.

Something I could not explain.

Now I see, it was I.

I was blaming others, but now this is my time to shed off the others.

There's hope of a future.

I believe in one where there's no competition.

I believe in a real one; not the kind others take a picture of for an Instagram post.

Everyone wants something to show.

What happened?

What era am I in?

JUST ASK.

If you have any questions, just ask.

"Part of me is missing, have you seen it?"

.

.

.

I have tough skin and since I choose not to boast it, does that mean I am wrong?

I have a powerful inner strength, but I choose not to flaunt it. Does that make me weak?

I do not give up, but I choose to do something differently with a greater impact. Does that make me indecisive and untrustworthy?

Everything I've chosen to do will be realized in a greater way rather than in pieces all over the internet.

I choose not to live my life in pieces; I do choose to live within the wholeness of my divinity despite what others think of me.

It has its challenges because I've done some things that may have made me come off as weak in the eyes of my brothers and sisters.

I did those things for my own eyes.

I did them to see within my own self.

I did not want to reveal myself in that way anymore.

I make my own decisions and not out of emotion, but through the creative energy that flows through the womb as well as the voice that pulls me out of my comfortable bed at dawn.

I've dedicated my life to honoring and researching ways to continue cultivating healing.

This is because the broken seek me for guidance.

I must prepare for this work even though I question the higher source as to why I am the one to do such a huge job.

There is so many things I do not innerstand about healing, but as I am. I gain confidence because I am human and a spiritual force.

Letting Go

It takes a lot of energy to release the baggage and to forgive.

What I am still learning is that love means to allow the other to live their life the way they decide without judgment, but it also holds them accountable.

I was surrounded by the wrong crowd when I realized how much of it was taking a toll on my mental health.

I have been blessed to be able to wake up strong and I now realize that I need to continue to follow through on my commitments for more than just myself, but life.

Every day is opening me up to this twisted reality of the world that I tried to make sense of for a long time. I needed a new crowd with different people to help me see what some of this was all about and what I truly felt I needed to do to help the community in a way that touches their hearts while changing their minds about the life they've continued to live.

I needed to let go and allow God to wash me clean.

Weary

I may cry, and I may sigh alone in my safe haven.
I'll keep rising and working hard.
Your friends and foes may roam the land.
You already knew where you belonged.
Have they been mean?
Dust it off.
Keep on protecting your heart; remember we're strong.

SWEET HEAVEN

Sweet Heaven

I long to go home.
The home in which the clouds hold,
or maybe the stars surrounding mars.
I want to go home.
I'm never done with this.
Meeting people feels like I'm getting close.
I'm antisocial, though it feels like the only fear I have to face.
Still, I realize I have a lot more work to do than I have clothes to choose.

EVE'S PERCEPTION

Eve's Perception

There was something wrong with the way I saw you.
I saw you as every man my mother had that treated her wrong.
There was something wrong with the way I saw myself.
I catch myself trying to grab onto silly things I used to like as a child.
I notice myself growing in ways I never knew.
I continue on my path hoping this longing does not shoot me dead.

...

...
What has my life become?
Caught in the rain yet again.
Trying to remain still,
I like how the rain sounds as it beats against my window seal.

GROWING UP

Growing Up

Growing pains.
Things are not what they seem.
People only dream about who they say they are.
Time keeps fading far.
Growing pains.
Small tasks seem large.
Emotionally drained.
I learned how to put my feelings away.
Growing pains.
Guys with cute smiles and repeating lies.
I guess I'm easy on the eyes.
Growing pains.
A vision apart from what the world really is in some places.
Growing pains.
Times are creeping up, and people are giving up.
Growing pains.

PROBLEMATIC

Problematic

A woman.
That was easy now wasn't it?
This word is one I struggle with.
To a man it means anything.
To a wo-man, what would it be?
The beauty in me reminds me that it can be far more than things I see.
Still this very thing baffles me.
Beauty runs in the genes.
I have hand-me-downs that don't fit well.
Ironic enough.
I had always been that chunky little girl with pants that were always too small for me.
I own scars,
tons of marks,
and a bruised heart.
Perhaps all they'll see is my beauty marks.

Little Lady

Dear young woman,
I'm talking to the ladies that love so hard.
The ones that see the good in those they love.
Stop believing you can save him.
Don't wait for him to show you love.
Open yourself up to it.
Dear young lady,
open your eyes.
Real love is felt everyday.
People or things will seem like love, but it's really an expression of your reflection.
And no I do not mean the one you see when you stare into the mirror for hours fixing yourself up to be rejected, neglected, and manipulated.
Harsh love? It's still love because I write with truth.
Put the phone down and raise up.
You're the divine power that helped God compile the mind up.
Dear young woman, wake up and allow yourself to be great.

Childish Things

Many of the women that call themselves mothers have told me that it is time to put childish things away.

I question what they mean as I watch their children watching themselves while the women are off parading different colored hair wigs, high volume eye lash extensions, and tons of makeup with foundation that is five times too bright to match their skin tone.

I also question the men that have judged me and have said similar things as they sit on their couches playing video games, or making strange remarks about bodacious women that enjoy showing off their beauty marks.

What is childish about the ways I've learned to rid my depression and anxiety?

I would paint and draw to reduce thoughts that hindered my writing abilities.

Call me crazy for going on walks for a breath of fresh air; perhaps I caught a contact high from all the marijuana being released in the air.

Yeah I may have sent things to someone I thought cared about me, but I did not go out having a baby without thinking to prepare how I wanted it to survive in this world.

Cultivating skills was my primary focus so that when I spent the time nurturing it, I would not have to serve anyone else or put my baby in the predicament to have the world toy with their mind.

Call it childish if you please; I'll always do me.

My child like nature does not at all stop me from my work, but being friendly is what got me to reverse.

I am forgetful; I will admit that.

What is so childish about wanting to remain in good health?

I was silly to believe someone else when they told me they loved me and now I have to continue believing in others just to make my way out of this part of the world.

How confusing this life.

I refuse to bring a child into this mess unless I work on continuing to change it and that I can say I have.

Paint me as a villain; go ahead and throw another "now hiring" ad in my face.

I'll throw it right back at you and hopefully it shakes some sense into your brain.

I'm fighting for my birthright, so stay focused on your second shift.

My life should not be of any concern to the way your family is going to live.

Watch your mouth and keep your feet on the ground.

All that gas you burn riding around the neighbor hood just going in circles is causing global warming yet you have the time to make comments about me and label them as warnings.

LOST

Lost

I watched you kiss me all gentle and slow motion.
It wasn't long before I fell into the ocean, drowning between your waves.
I resisted the urge to save myself.
I began falling in love with your ways.
I let it carry me without worrying about whether or not I'd be safe because I knew I was.

FIELD OF FLOWERS

Field of Flowers

She's like a sunflower, so beautiful and full of seed.

She arises at dawn, works, studies, and plays.

The sun sets, still she wonders.

Stars twinkle, hearts mingle and still, she watches the very existence of time crush minds that like to clock out and whisper petty punchlines.

Wondering who she is to say a certain way is the best way.

She just wants to see you through, alive, and happy.

Sweet flowers fill the edges of her mind, cuddling her with the very magical existence of time.

This thing about time has got her on the edge of her chair.

She is wondering what she needs to be doing for her creator, so she's up at dawn asking Him for guidance.

She asks for a sign to what is right.

She still smells the flowers;

Possibly this is what is right.

Her standing right in the middle.

Untouched.

Curses

These things will leave you dead;
Grasping onto life with both hands.
I remind myself not to slip because the enemy likes to play tricks.
They pretend to care, they pretend to be all of these things you want, but it isn't anything you truly need.
They pretend to be you and they will create things to break you down.
It's a death sentence, but you must continue rising up and remembering that God is the only source that can provide a way out of the dark.
Men and women will greet you with smiles behind desperation and deception; still, you must allow God to work within you.
Curses are spoken over the land and it interrupts your mind to focus on the gift God planned in you.
Recognize this immediately.
Curses.
Do your best to overcome everything with a strong heart.
Smile because you're alive.
Shout your praise no matter how loud and walk with your head up.
Eyes on the sky.
Your timing is perfect;
You're everything we need.
Curses will have you living like others.
Dressing like others.
We're all looking for the same thing, a way out of this hell.
Well let me remind you to continue looking within yourself.

COMMUNITY

Community

My neighborhood is cool.

Every child that walks by wants to greet my dog, Blue.

They tell me things and I promise to keep their secrets, but in return I offer them a piece of advice that'll allow them to go far along with the love and protection of their families.

They're so creative, talented, and funny.

I have spared some time with them to get them thinking on better things.

I see them coming out to play, so I pray that God continues to keep them safe.

Some of their families are broken and they do not yet know what could be at stake.

What's happened to some of our communities?

An old English teacher reminded me that it was just something that I had been born into.

It's worse when we're searching for something that was already inside of us the entire time.

I thought it was all the same but then I got to know my brain.

Serve within your community, and do not be afraid to show your face or lend them your name.

Fear God, only he can continue to sculpt you and provide a better way.

After all how free are you if you're the only one behind the gates?

Our mothers and fathers may doubt our dreams or struggle to listen that is why I remind the children to strive and follow what their souls are telling them.

It's never too late and I know they have not let it go.

People have told me that Saginaw is boring and there is nothing here.

I would then glance at them wondering about their insides.

Something was telling me that perhaps they were unaware that they're only spiritually living here.

Their mind has been toyed with and their hearts have been too trusting, I've also been there.

It's important for them to think again.

It is a cycle that their children will only repeat.

We must forgive in order to understand.

We will cry, but continue to envision a better tomorrow for the future.

Be strong for our babies.

They're still learning to understand.

IN WRITING

In Writing

Poetry is a foundation that has transformed me.

Life moves on like we do, next thing I know I'm gray complaining about the same folks.

Here I learn to let go.

Poetry is something I must continue to unlearn.

It is in my own writing that reminds me to continuously keep learning.

I often notice myself being forgetful about keeping up with the things I love.

Does this count me out?

Who is to blame if there is no one around?

Rather than blaming myself, I like to try again without the distractions of my people getting in the way.

Sometimes I pretend to run away and stop at the corner because I realize I can do more with this struggle.

I'm getting better I say to myself.

Every day is a brand new one and I am breathing fresh air.

I am thankful to have learned how to properly care in such a way that makes my life peaceful beyond measure.

It is hard, yes and I mess it up occasionally.

I feel guilty when I struggle to keep up with my own anxiety because in this world I will need to make my voice sounder, and this frightens me.

I do not have any doubt and I despise fear.

I'll run it out.

Poetry has transformed me, so I write even if I have nothing to share.

LONGING FOR MY LOVE

Longing for my love

I rest my head hoping to get through the night without wanting you on my mind.
I wait for the day we can soon embrace each other.
I miss those moments when it felt okay.
Missing all the nights we walked together even in the rain.
I apologize for feeling as if I need you.
I know you feel it when I tell you I love you.
I mean it and you see it.
I'm inconsistent; I fear commitment, but I still lack resistance when it comes to you.
You're the moon in my eyes, beautiful yet painfully full and visible on a certain day... no surprise.
Our kisses unlock doors to worlds unknown.
I have hoped you find your way back to me even knowing you have other places to be.
Come feel me, let's create memories.

Family Reunion

In my defense, I cannot recall ever really reuniting with them.

They were strangers that continued to change.

I was afraid to try strange food they made.

Perhaps it had been trauma from the intense stomach pains.

The old folks told stories about the family, and I loved to listen because they were funny.

My great grandmother reminds me to stay sweet.

I smile with grace, because I've envisioned some pain.

I've also encountered some deceit.

My heart remains solid for them because I realize I'll become a different version.

It is because of them that I remain proud of my genes.

People laugh at me and may even judge my family.

It does not bother me anymore.

The next family gathering I promised myself I wouldn't be so shy or afraid of what they'll say about the things I am working on.

That is if we'll ever decide to have one.

Even though some would rather leave quickly to resume the other relationships they have labeled as family.

We were always somewhat divided, so I sat quietly at the little table with my milkshake and fries wondering why.

Now there are new members and they made babies with glowing eyes.

I glance at them and smile slightly because I know when they grow bigger they'll change lives.

I just hope they continue receiving the love they need for them to grow strong.

No more being raised by television screens, or manipulating acts of "real" love.

Play to Win

The world is a play and we are the actors.
If you are to be anything in this world,
Be you without the voices running up beside you trying to turn you around.
Be yourself through the hard parts.
Cast your soul, your worries, and your cares upon God.
He hears you in the voids.
Do not be lost in the noise.
Keep running.
You're a winner and they'll make you feel like a loser just to get you back once you've realized who you are.
Play to win because you were standing on a throne from the very time of your birth.
You'll never need to beg for a thing.
I promise you,
Play to win even if you lose over and over again.
That's how this game of life goes.
Failure is not the end,
It is the beginning.
Play to win.
Your soul will be redeemed and your heart will be made whole.
Stand strong and own your DNA.

DECIDE

Decide

You have the power to make a decision for your own life.
You choose the route.
Change the things you can control.
Do not worry about the things you cannot.
Decide that no one can disturb your peace any longer.
No Q&A's.
Decide.
Stick to your decisions and rise up every day to them.
Yes, it is hard, but I write to remind you that it'll get easier.
Once you decide,
You'll never have to settle for an average life.
No one can come and control you.
Decide what it is and what it will not be.
Do not be afraid to speak that and stand up for yourself.
A lot of people will run away and try to throw things your way.
They will even try to keep you in fear.
You're stronger than illusions.
You're stronger than conceptual difficulties.
You're even stronger than your own patterns.
Do not be afraid to morph into that butterfly.
Decide to let it be.
Allow it to spread its wings.
Decide to be the gardener in your own field of flowers.
No one else will tend them the way you know how.

CPSIA information can be obtained
at www.ICGtesting.com
Printed in the USA
BVHW011230040121
596934BV00010B/288